GUIDELINES

W9-CFS-339

Christian education

Planning for Lifelong Faith Formation

Carol F. Krau
General Board of Discipleship

CHRISTIAN EDUCATION

Copyright © 2008 by Cokesbury

This book is printed on acid-free paper.

ISBN 978-0-687-64941-9

Some paragraph numbers for and language in the Book of Discipline *may have changed in the 2008 revision, which was published after these Guidelines were printed. We regret any inconvenience.*

MANUFACTURED IN THE UNITED STATES OF AMERICA

Contents

Welcome

Y
ou are so important to the life of the Christian church! You have consented to join with other people of faith who, through the millennia, have sustained the church by extending God's love to others.

You have been called and have committed your unique passions, gifts, and abilities to a position of leadership. This Guideline will help you understand the basic elements of that ministry within your own church and within The United Methodist Church.

Called to Spiritual Leadership

Each person is called to ministry by virtue of his or her baptism, and that ministry takes place in all aspects of daily life, in and outside the church. As a pastoral leader or leader among the laity, your ministry is not just a "job," but a spiritual endeavor. You *are* a spiritual leader now, and others will look to you for spiritual leadership. What does this mean?

First, *all* persons who follow Jesus are called to grow spiritually through the practice of various Christian habits (or "means of grace") such as prayer, Bible study, private and corporate worship, acts of service, Christian conferencing, and so on. Jesus taught his disciples practices of spiritual growth and leadership that you, as a disciple, are to share with others as they look to you to be a model and guide.

Second, it means that you always keep your eye on the main reasons for any ministry—to help others grow to a mature faith in God that moves them to action on behalf of others, especially "the least" (see Matthew 25:31-46). This is an aspect of "disciple making," which is the ultimate goal of all that we do in the church.

CULTIVATING VISION AND MISSION

As a spiritual leader, a primary function you carry is to help those you lead to see as clearly as possible what God is calling your church to be and to do. Ideally, your church council first forms this vision and then forms plans and goals for how to fulfill that vision. As a leader, you will help your team remain focused and accountable to honor the vision and goals to which the church is committed. You will help your team create and evaluate suggestions, plans, and activities against the measure: *Does this move us closer to our church's vision to bring others to God in this place and time?*

CHRISTIAN CONFERENCING

While there are appropriate and useful business-like practices that apply to church life, Christian practices distinguish the church as the church. In the United Methodist tradition, how we meet and work together is important. "Christian Conferencing" involves listening not only to each other, but also listening intently for the will of God in any given task or conversation. This makes prayer essential in the midst of "business as usual." As Christians, we are called to "speak the truth in love." This is a special way to speak in which we treat one another as if each of us were Christ among us. As a spiritual leader in your ministry area, you have the privilege and opportunity to teach and model these practices. By remembering that each of us is beloved of God and discerning the presence of God in all that the church does, every task becomes worshipful work.

THE MISSION OF THE UNITED METHODIST CHURCH

The United Methodist Church is a connectional church, which means in part that every local church is interrelated through the structure and organization of districts, conferences, jurisdictions, and central conferences in the larger "family" of the denomination. *The Book of Discipline of The United Methodist Church* describes, among other things, the ministry of all United Methodist Christians, the essence of servant ministry and leadership, how to organize and accomplish that ministry, and how our connectional structure works (see especially ¶¶125–138).

Our Church is more than a structure; it is a living organism. The *Discipline* describes our mission to proclaim the gospel and to welcome people into the body of Christ, to lead people to a commitment to God through Jesus Christ, to nurture them in Christian living by various means of grace, and to send persons into the world as agents of Jesus Christ (¶122). Thus, through you—and many other Christians—this very relational mission continues.

(For help in addition to this Guideline and the *Book of Discipline*, see "Resources" at the end of your Guideline, www.umc.org, and the other websites listed on the inside back cover.)

What Is Our Purpose?

imagine what your faith life would be like if you had never attended Sunday school, read your Bible, or experienced any other group that explored the Scriptures. You would only know the faith stories by way of the short selections of Scriptures read during worship and from conversation with others. Education—learning—undergirds everything we do and is a firm foundation in the life of faithful discipleship, yet it is more than that. At its best, Christian education is about information, formation, and transformation.

We see early in the Old Testament that teaching and learning are important. Parents are urged to teach their children about the great events and acts of God and their meaning for the faith community (Deuteronomy 6). Wisdom, that is, learning and living a righteous life, is extolled in the Wisdom literature, particularly in Proverbs (for example, 1:1-7; 4:1-27). Jesus, among other attributes, was a masterful teacher, using parables and other illustrations to convey his message of salvation. In all of these instances, *knowing* is necessary, but the point is related to *being*. We gain information so that we may be formed into the likeness of Christ, and through that experience, we become God's agents of transformation in the world (see, for example, Romans 12).

As a leader in your congregation, you are in charge of planning and implementing experiences through which children, youth, and adults come to know God and discover ways to live as Christian disciples. Your number one responsibility is to keep this purpose before the congregation through all that you do. Every class and small group should recognize that its purpose is to support the formation of Christian faith and discipleship in its participants. This purpose sets the church apart from other community organizations and activities.

The Mission of the Church

United Methodists take discipleship seriously! The General Conference of The United Methodist Church has clearly identified our denominational mission: To make disciples of Jesus Christ for the transformation of the world (*The Book of Discipline of The United Methodist Church,* 2008, ¶120). The process for carrying out this mission is described as:
- proclaim the gospel; seek, welcome, and gather persons into the body of Christ
- lead persons to commit their lives to God through baptism by water and the spirit and profession of faith in Jesus Christ

- nurture persons in Christian living through worship, the sacraments, spiritual disciplines, and other means of grace, such as Wesley's Christian conferencing
- send persons into the world to live lovingly and justly as servants of Christ by healing the sick; feeding the hungry; caring for the stranger; freeing the oppressed; being and becoming a compassionate, caring presence; and working to develop social structures that are consistent with the gospel; and
- continue the mission of seeking, welcoming, and gathering persons into the community of the body of Christ (*Discipline,* ¶122).

Sunday school is one setting in which this mission takes place, but it is not the whole picture. Every group and class contributes to the ministry of Christian education and formation for the nurture of the church. Each class and group serves the mission of the church by being a place for welcoming, for inviting commitment, and for equipping for ministry, as well as for teaching, learning, and practicing spiritual disciplines.

Christian Education Is Christian Formation

There are a number of different small group settings in which Christian formation occurs. Regardless of the setting, these groups share a common purpose. This purpose is explored in *Foundations: Shaping the Ministry of Christian Education in Your Congregation* (see Resources). In short, this purpose states: Through Christian education, we invite people and communities of faith to be transformed as they are inspired and challenged to:
- know and experience God through Jesus Christ
- claim and live God's promises
- grow and serve as Christian disciples.

THE MEANS OF GRACE

Throughout the centuries, Christians have discovered spiritual practices that have helped them know God. John Wesley called these practices *means of grace*—means by which we experience God's grace. Wesley's classes supported members in using these spiritual practices and in deepening their faith and practice. These spiritual practices include:
- prayer
- study of the Scriptures
- worship (especially celebrating the Lord's Supper)
- fasting
- Christian conversation
- works of mercy (showing compassion and working for justice).

Your educational ministries should help persons learn to use these spiritual disciplines. It is not enough to know *about* prayer—we need to pray. It is not enough to know *about* the Bible—we need to incorporate its wisdom and truth into our daily living. It is not enough to know *about* worship—our lives should be shaped by the reality of God's presence and, therefore, be filled with joy and praise.

Of equal importance is the flow of your classes and groups. If the task is to help persons grow and mature in faith and discipleship, then the classes and group experiences need to be structured in a way that provides a progression for greater depth and commitment, rather than offering only a collection of studies, books, or other disconnected activities. This level of intentionality places responsibility on you and on the teachers and leaders you recruit to have a well-planned system of education and formation ministry.

People in your congregation, including members of your ministry team, will have had varied experience with Christian education. Some will have attended Sunday school since childhood; others may have never participated in a class or small group. Most will be somewhere in between those two ends of the spectrum. It is better not to assume that everyone understands the purpose of Christian education in the same way. You may find that people have quite different perspectives about what you're trying to accomplish. Your work will be more effective if you spend time exploring your purpose, praying, and building a shared vision for your educational ministries, first with your teachers and other education leaders, and then with the congregation.

THE PASTOR AS ADVOCATE AND EDUCATOR

It is impossible to overestimate the role of the pastor as a teacher and as an advocate for the ministry of Christian education and formation. For better or worse, the ministries that the pastoral leader emphasizes and advocates for assume a greater sense of value in the congregation. The pastoral leader, especially in small membership churches, may be the only one with specialized training in theology, Scripture study, and other facets of the church, which places some responsibility on him or her to share the benefit of that education with the rest of the congregation.

Getting Started

a s you plan and organize, you will work closely with your pastor and the church council to align your work with the mission of the congregation. You may also work with an education or nurture ministry team, a Sunday school superintendent, a small group coordinator, a spiritual formation chairperson, and age-level coordinators. In smaller membership churches, your team may consist of you and the other teachers.

Basic Responsibilities

The basic responsibilities you carry as the chairperson of the education committee or coordinator of educational ministries are to:

- listen to God through worship, prayer, Bible study, and conversation with Christian friends to discern God's call for your congregation
- listen to people in order to determine needs and to develop opportunities that help them strengthen their relationship with God and respond through Christian discipleship
- convene the ministry team for Christian education and/or nurture
- work with your pastor and the ministry team to build and interpret a congregational vision for Christian education and formation
- assess needs, identify gaps, and set priorities for your congregation's ministries of Christian formation
- plan, monitor, and evaluate settings and ministries for teaching, learning, and practicing spiritual disciplines for persons of all ages
- identify and equip effective leaders for each class or small group
- identify needed resources for each group
- develop and administer the annual education budget.

TIP: Listening to people will help you connect the work of the congregation with the hopes and dreams of the people you serve. Talk to parents, children, young people, and other adults in the classes, congregation, and community, and encourage your teachers to do the same. Ask open-ended questions, such as "Tell me about your experience in this congregation" and jot down notes as you learn. After several conversations, review what you have heard and look for patterns and themes. Use this information as you plan.

Relating to Other Education Leaders

The size of your congregation often determines the number and organization of leaders with responsibility for Christian education and formation and/or age-level ministries. Generally speaking, the larger the congregation, the greater the number of leaders needed. These leaders may include a Sunday school superintendent, a small group ministries coordinator, any age-level coordinators, a spiritual formation coordinator, and others determined by your congregation. If you attend a very small congregation, your title may be different from "chairperson of education," but your responsibilities are generally described in this Guideline. Your team may be the teachers and/or other volunteers.

These leaders may assist in planning so that all ministries of Christian education and formation support one another and operate from the same understanding of the congregation's mission. Together you are responsible for carrying out or delegating such tasks as:
- promoting opportunities for learning and spiritual formation
- supervising the Sunday school and age-level ministries
- organizing and implementing weekday ministries
- planning events, such as vacation Bible school or seasonal activities
- providing ongoing opportunities for teachers to build knowledge and skills
- ordering curriculum resources and purchasing supplies and equipment
- maintaining safe, clean, and attractive facilities
- maintaining records of attendance and leadership for the classes and groups that will be counted in the annual statistical reports.

Beginning Your Work

Pray for your team, your pastor, and your congregation. Ask that God will guide your leadership and focus the work of the ministry team.

Survey all the classes and groups to be sure you know about all of them. Most will be organized classes on Sundays or weekdays; others may be informal or occasional groups that meet away from the church.

Talk with your pastor and other leaders about the mission and vision of your congregation. Learn how the classes and small groups for Christian formation and discipleship support the mission and vision.

Identify resources that can support your leadership (page 31). Contact your conference office to see who provides leadership for Christian education in the annual conference and in your district. Ask to be put on the mailing list to receive Christian education information along with your conference and district newsletters. Check the websites within the denomination for other resource helps.

Call each ministry team member to introduce yourself to the members who are not acquainted with you and to welcome new team members. Talk with team members about their particular area of responsibility—what they hope to accomplish, how their work fits into the overall vision for Christian education and formation, and how you can support their ministry.

Convene a meeting of the team within thirty days of the beginning of the planning year. Your goals will be to get acquainted, to explore the purpose of your ministry, and to acquaint team members with the current plan for educational ministries.

Identify needed learning for you and your team members. Include other congregational leaders with whom you need to be acquainted.

Begin prioritizing work that needs to be done in the coming months. Clarify responsibilities and timelines for the various team members' work.

TIP: You may have other new persons on the team. Make sure that they have a copy of the Guidelines related to their area of responsibility. (See back cover for a list of titles.) You may also want to read copies of Guidelines related to age-level ministries so that you better understand how the work of age-level ministries relates to the ministry of Christian education and formation.

Creating an Effective Team

Pray and study the Scriptures together in your team meetings. Include group-building activities such as storytelling and sharing joys and concerns.

Discuss how your different responsibilities work together to accomplish the purpose of Christian education and formation. Ask team members to state what kind of support they need from one another in order to be effective.

Recognize and celebrate the gifts and abilities of each team member. Express your appreciation for the contribution of each team member. Draw on the strengths of each person as you plan. Ask team members to take responsibility for leading parts of the agenda.

Create a meeting climate of respect and trust. Encourage different ideas and opinions. Ask questions to help the team explore assumptions, values, and likely outcomes for possibilities under consideration. Consider forming a covenant among yourselves to remind yourself of your commitments.

Include times for reflection and discernment. Use these times to discuss how faithfully and effectively your work is accomplishing what you hope to accomplish. Ask questions about how you can improve what you are doing.

Planning Ministry Team Meetings

Before the Meeting
- Check the date and time to avoid conflicts with activities of other important congregational groups.
- Prepare the agenda for the meeting.
- Give team members the date, time, place, agenda, and other materials far enough in advance so that they can prepare to participate actively.
- Contact the church office if you have special needs related to room arrangement or equipment.

At the Meeting
- Begin on time.
- Designate a person to keep track of decisions, assignments, and deadlines. Provide for balanced participation by persons of various viewpoints.
- Adjust the agenda so that priority items receive adequate attention.
- Ask for feedback on the effectiveness of the meeting so that you can incorporate helpful suggestions into future team meetings.

After the Meeting
- Promptly review your notes on decisions and assignments to make sure they are clear and accurate.
- Send out minutes to remind others of the assignments they accepted.
- Check on progress with people working on assignments.
- Thank persons who have provided special resources or assistance.
- Reflect on the decisions and plans in light of the vision and goals of the congregation so that the group may continue on course. Think about additional information the team needs to continue with plans.
- Begin building the agenda for the next meeting.

Relating to Other Groups in the Church

CHURCHWIDE PLANNING AND ADMINISTRATION
1. The Charge Conference. The charge conference meets annually and is the primary administrative body in the local church. The members of the charge conference are generally also members of the church council. It sets policy, approves the annual budget, endorses the direction for the ministries of the congregation, and elects persons to leadership positions. You may report about educational ministries to the charge conference and receive guidance from the charge conference related to congregational priorities for small group ministries and discipleship formation.

2. The Church Council. The church council or the equivalent structure in your congregation (such as the council on ministries) is responsible for planning and coordinating the congregation's ministries. This body ensures that every aspect of the church's mission is adequately planned and supported. You are a member of the church council. You keep the council apprised of your ministry team's plans and needs.

MINISTRY DEVELOPMENT AND SUPPORT LEVEL
3. The Ministry Team for Christian Education and Formation (or Nurture). Smaller congregations may organize the ministry of Christian education and formation under the broader arena of nurture ministry. Members of this ministry team plan for the full spectrum of the congregation's needs: children, youth, families, single adults, teachers, persons with special needs, and others. The pastor, along with any Christian education staff, serves as an ex officio member of the ministry team. The team builds a congregational system for teaching and learning that addresses these needs comprehensively. The church council elects the members of the team.

4. Age-Level and Life-Span Ministries. Larger congregations may need a mid-level of organization; the church council may elect age-level coordinators and age-level council members to serve as chairpersons of the age-level councils. Age-level and life-span ministries may consist of one or more coordinators, one or more councils (leadership teams), or a combination of coordinators and councils. Each coordinator or council acts as an advocate for a certain group in the church, for example, families or older adults.

PROGRAM IMPLEMENTATION LEVEL
5. The Sunday School and Small Group Ministries. The Sunday school and small group ministries are mandated parts of the local church (*Discipline* ¶252.2a). These ministries operate under the guidance of leadership designated by the church council. These ministries enable persons to experience God's presence, build knowledge and skills for discipleship, receive and express support, and participate in service in Christ's name.

THE WHOLE PICTURE
The charge conference sets the vision and direction for the ministry of the church, which is implemented by the church council. The church council gives oversight and direction to the education or nurture committee and age-level / life-span ministry areas, if any. Within the education and age-level areas, specific plans are created and implemented, and those goals and results are considered at the church council.

Planning for Christian Education and Formation
What Do I Plan?

the process of transformation is indeed the goal of your ministry. This process involves developing and strengthening skills, identifying and shaping values, building knowledge, and experiencing a supportive Christian community. Our denomination understands this process as *sanctification*—going on to perfection. As our experience of God deepens, we become more Christlike. We mature in faith and develop a coherence of belief and behavior.

Your congregation is unique. Therefore, as you plan with your goal in mind, the settings, the content, and the particular details related to each educational opportunity should be designed to match your congregation. As you and your team work together to determine the exact ministries needed in your congregation, however, you may want to reflect on how your congregation assists persons to grow and mature in the following areas:

Knowledge of the Bible
- Old Testament
- New Testament
- Major biblical persons, events, and themes

Skills Related to Learning the Bible
- Methods of Bible study
- Resources for Bible study (concordances, atlases, dictionaries, and so forth)

Knowledge of the Church
- Christian worship
- United Methodist heritage
- Christian sacraments (baptism and Holy Communion)
- Other sacramental events that deal with "rites of passage," such as confirmation, funerals, and weddings
- Understanding of the meaning and flow of the Christian year
- Church structure and organization (local church, district, and annual conference)

Spiritual Formation
- Methods for prayer
- Bible study skills
- Fasting
- Participation in worship
- Ability to share faith stories
- Knowing stories of the "saints"
- Other spiritual disciplines, such as Christian conversation

Knowledge for Connecting Faith and Daily Life
- Understanding how to apply biblical principles in everyday life
- Building healthy families and communities
- Incorporating ethics in the workplace
- Knowing issues affecting your community, the nation, and the world
- Participating in mission and outreach
- Working for peace and justice

Skills for Connecting Faith and Daily Life
- Recognizing assumptions
- Identifying and evaluating options
- Reflecting on personal experience in light of Scripture and tradition
- Making decisions consistent with values and beliefs

Forming Values and Characteristics Consistent With the Gospel
- Compassion
- Generosity
- Mercy
- Hope
- Loving-kindness
- Self-control
- Peace
- Joy
- Hospitality
- Patience

As you can see, there is a balance among knowing, experiencing, doing, and relating, which are all facets of mature faith development. What else might you add to or change on this list? Are there areas in which you are quite strong, but weak in others? Talk with your team about how you plan for children, youth, and adults in order to develop these skills, knowledge, values, and experience. Review and evaluate your current ministries in light of this conversation. Identify gaps and priorities for planning future ministries.

For Whom Do I Plan?
God is calling your congregation to ministry with God's people. God's people in your community include persons who are of certain ages, who are employed in various occupations, and who come from particular cultural heritages. Through Christian education, these specific people come to recognize themselves as a part of all God's people, who extend beyond your community.

As you plan, focus on people and their relationships with God and one another. Start with people and plan ministries that address their real-life needs instead of planning ministries and then finding ways to fit people into them. The first way of planning is relationally focused; the latter method is institutionally focused. You are not trying to maintain an institution; you are working to connect people with the risen Lord!

Knowing as much as possible about the people in and around your congregation will help you set priorities, determine new settings for ministry, and reach out to new people. Who are the people in your congregation and in your community? What are their needs? their gifts? Perhaps you will find:
- children whose parents are at work when they come home from school
- single adults with no family nearby
- middle-aged adults caring for aging parents
- persons with physical and mental disabilities
- young people who hunger for a meaningful relationship with an adult
- senior adults who are coping with retirement or the loss of a spouse.

As you get to know these people, you will also find that they have different preferred ways of learning, just as your teachers will have preferred ways to teach. For the most effective ministry of education and formation, you will want to be sure your teachers are acquainted with these multiple intelligences. (See the Resources section.)

How Do I Plan?

Be clear about what you're trying to accomplish. As your team continues to pray, study, and work together, develop a mental picture of what your congregation would be like if it were preparing and supporting persons faithfully and effectively in living as disciples of Jesus Christ. Invite as many individuals and groups as possible to provide feedback and input for this vision.

Think about your congregation and your community. Then review your current classes and small groups. Identify which groups provide "entry points" into the congregation. Assess which groups provide basic information about the Christian faith and which groups invite people into a deeper relationship with God. As has been mentioned before, one expectation of your area of ministry is that it will help people move through the various stages of faith toward greater maturity. One level of assessment will involve knowing what faith formation needs are met by existing groups and how well you help people move into new settings that enable growth.

Make a list of your strengths and your gaps in ministry. Be honest about the programs that are no longer effective in helping persons grow in faith. With the proper "leave-taking" it is possible to honor the contributions of groups that had once been vital and then retire them or direct them to something new.

A third level of assessment is in identifying what is missing, especially if existing groups are ended. What age levels or Christian education and formation needs are currently unrecognized or require more attention? Are there other special needs groups that could be formed under the ministry of Christian education? (If you have a small group ministries coordinator, how might you work together?)

Recognize points at which you need to do some research or additional learning. Spend time listening to persons in the congregation. Read and discuss a book together. Meet with a leader who can help you learn about the changes taking place in your community and society at large, then develop new strategies for Christian formation in today's context.

Explore alternatives. Be open to new ideas. Learn what other congregations are doing to develop Christian disciples. At this stage, avoid "we've always done it that way" and "it'll never work" thinking. Recognize your own unique identity and setting as a congregation, rather than copying or importing in whole the ministry model of another church. Evaluate instead the success factors that can be replicated or adapted to your church.

Decide which possibilities will be most effective in moving your congregation toward its vision. Set priorities related to what needs to be done first, next, and so on. Determine a timeline for your work so that you can measure your progress and readjust plans when necessary.

Develop an action plan. Clarify all the details for each educational opportunity. Include information related to the following:
- biblical/ theological purpose
- target audience
- date, time, and location
- leadership
- resources and equipment
- room setup
- publicity
- budget
- evaluation.

Establish a feedback loop. Use surveys, questionnaires, and other means to receive feedback from leaders and participants in each setting. Use the feedback to plan more effectively, to build on your strengths, and to eliminate unnecessary work.

Celebrate your ministry. In your ministry team meetings, have a party to celebrate the conclusion of a special event. Send a note of thanks to Sunday school teachers and other group leaders. During worship, invite the members of the congregation to give thanks for what they are learning and for how they are growing in faith. Enlist the aid of your pastoral leader to both celebrate and advocate for this ministry.

TIP: You can develop a standard feedback form to be used with your youth and adult classes or groups. At the top of the form, include a space for entering the name of the group or setting, as well as the location and times of the meetings. Then provide several questions for reflection, with space for written responses. Use questions such as:
- What did you learn (or experience)?
- What was most helpful about this opportunity?
- How will you use what you learned and experienced?
- What are your suggestions for the next time this opportunity is offered?
- In what additional ways can this congregation support you in living as a disciple of Jesus Christ?

When Do I Plan?

Planning is an ongoing process. Advance planning may be done yearly, quarterly, or monthly. The type of learning opportunity and time needed to prepare for it determine how far in advance you should begin.

The "Monthly Planning Guide" on the CD-ROM accompanying the full set of Guidelines and on the GBOD website (www.gbod.org/education) suggests a possible flow based on the calendar year. Depending on your meeting schedule, combine tasks as necessary. You may want to meet monthly if your team is new so that the team can learn its responsibilities and receive needed support and guidance.

Each quarter you will want to finalize plans for events and classes taking place that quarter. In addition, you will begin planning for events and learning opportunities scheduled for the next three months.

TIP: Plan early enough to be able to confirm with the church council that your plans conform to the overall direction that the council has set. Remember also to check the church calendar when scheduling events in order to avoid conflicting with other church programming that involves the same people you want included in your event. As soon as your dates are confirmed, call the church office to place the dates on the church calendar. If the church calendar tends to fill up quickly, consider getting a list of open dates immediately *before* a planning session so that you schedule your events on days that can accommodate your plans.

Budgeting for Christian Education

Y ou are responsible for developing and overseeing the budget for educational ministries in your congregation. You will submit an annual budget request to the committee on finance. The charge conference will approve the final budget. Categories frequently found in the education budget include:

- curriculum resources
- books, videos, and DVDs
- supplies
- new equipment
- equipment maintenance
- registration fees for leadership development events
- food or gifts to express appreciation for teachers and group leaders.

TIP: **(1)** Ask your pastor, the chairperson of the finance committee, or the church treasurer to give you copies of the budget for last year and this year. Check the estimated needs against actual expenses to determine adjustments for the coming year. **(2)** If your congregation has a children's or youth choir, preschool, day care, or parents' day out programs, consult with those leaders to determine budget needs and who will request them.

During the year, when requesting funds or making purchases for something expensive (however your congregation defines that) check with the church treasurer to be sure that he or she knows a bill is coming and that the budget is equipped to handle it. Money in the budget is not the same as money in the bank. The book *The Ministry of Christian Education and Formation* has a chapter devoted to budget and finance. *Vital Ministry in the Small Membership Church: Christian Education* will be especially helpful for churches with modest budgets. See Resources.

Each congregation is responsible for deciding how to build a budget. Your budget may include only the items listed above related to Sunday school and teachers' meetings. If you need to budget for all items related to age-level ministries, you may include funds for programs, such as:

- vacation Bible school
- weekday ministries
- youth group(s)
- senior adult ministries
- mission education
- retreats
- special events for the liturgical year, such as an Advent workshop.

One other consideration, in consultation with the staff/pastor-parish relations committee and the children's and youth ministry leaders, is the expense for background checks for staff and volunteers who work with minors or vulnerable adults. **Background checks should be considered mandatory, no matter what size your church or education ministry.**

Developing Effective Teachers

the Book of Acts (8:26-40) tells the story of Philip meeting an Ethiopian official who was reading from the Book of Isaiah. When Philip asked the man if he understood what he was reading, the man replied, "How can I, unless someone guides me?" The story then says that Philip "began to speak, and starting with this Scripture, he proclaimed to him the good news about Jesus." As a result of their meeting, the Ethiopian official was baptized.

This brief story illustrates the importance of teachers in the faith formation of persons. It is not unusual for persons to name a Sunday school teacher from years ago as one of the most significant influences in shaping their faith. Teachers serve as interpreters of Scripture and spiritual mentors. They stimulate thought, encourage Christian values, and help develop decision-making skills. They become true "friends in faith." Whether they realize it or not, all leaders in Christian education and formation (and other ministry leaders as well) are spiritual leaders. The children and others will look up to you and to their teachers as models, so the question is not whether you are a spiritual leader, but rather, What kind of spiritual leader are you?

Critical Processes for Effective Teachers

Teachers are vital to accomplishing the goals of your educational ministries. In order for people to experience the transforming presence of God, their teachers need knowledge and skill in several critical processes:
- keeping in touch with God—developing a relationship with God through the spiritual disciplines
- keeping in touch with God's people—listening intently to the hopes and dreams of persons in their class or group, understanding any special needs, and accommodating diverse learning styles
- keeping in touch with experience—reflecting on family, work, and society in light of Scripture and tradition
- keeping in touch with the world—participating in the ongoing mission and ministry of the church
- keeping in touch with teaching—developing the ability to use a variety of teaching methods and resources.
- keeping an open mind—being willing to entertain "wild" questions or comments without judgment or censure
- keeping a sense of humor—a must when dealing with children, youth, and volunteers!

As your ministry team identifies persons with the gifts and skills for teaching, you will want to support them by encouraging their spiritual growth and by equipping them with the skills and knowledge they need to teach effectively. Talk with teachers to find out how you can provide support for individual and small group reflection, discernment, and learning.

> **TIP:** New teachers will benefit from the wisdom of experienced teachers. Ask one of your strong teachers to mentor a new teacher. Consider establishing teacher apprentices by teaming an inexperienced teacher with an experienced teacher. Invite effective teachers to lead workshops on teaching methods and share ideas with new teachers.

Identifying Teachers

Pray. Begin by praying for God's guidance. Ask for wisdom in discerning whom God would call.

Work as a team. Ask other members of the ministry team, the Sunday school superintendent, members of the committee on lay leadership, and/or the pastor to help with this ongoing task. Review needs several times during the year.

Assess your needs. In what settings are teachers or group leaders needed? Will those presently teaching continue to do so? Prepare a chart listing all classes and positions. Allow space for noting who will contact each person, when, and what response was received. (Include substitutes and any team-teaching possibilities.)

Develop a job description for teachers. Include this information:
- Name and ages of the class or group
- Time, date, and location of the class or group
- Specific responsibilities for leading this class or group
- Abilities and knowledge needed
- Time involvement and requested length of commitment.

Formulate policies to screen all volunteer or paid leadership with children, youth and vulnerable adults. Be clear that these policies communicate and support our belief in the sanctity of human life. State how these policies protect adult leadership as well as children and youth. (Refer to *Safe Sanctuaries*, listed in Resources.)

Establish expectations. Review the critical processes for effective teaching and your vision for Christian education. Discuss what you expect from teachers and what they can expect from the congregation. One minimal expectation is that teachers and other volunteers in a classroom will at least do no harm. Check the *Comprehensive Plan for Teacher Development* at www.gbod.org/education/resources for a very helpful continuum on what teachers need to know and be able to do.

Identify potential teachers and leaders. Make a list of persons with the gifts for teaching. Include people who can develop these gifts and those who already possess them. Ask your pastor, congregation, and class members for input. There is a great appeal to an adult knowing that children or youth have specifically requested them.

Inviting Teachers

Ask people to teach. Talk with each person individually. If you send a letter of invitation, follow up with a personal conversation.

Explain the responsibilities and expectations. Talk about your congregation's vision for Christian education as it relates to the formation of Christian disciples. Make a connection between this vision and the role teachers play in helping your congregation move toward its vision. Be clear about the expectations and lines of accountability. Indicate if teachers are expected to attend regular training events or take a class themselves from time to time. Identify who teachers notify if they must be absent and what to do in emergencies.

> **TIP:** If you're visiting with a person who has never taught before, bring along a sample of the resources used in the group. Point out the features that will assist him or her in preparing to lead and describe the group. If there is a teaching team, share information about the team members. Better yet, have the other teachers visit with you so you can speak to the whole team at once.

Describe and call forth the person's gifts. Explain why you believe she or he is the right leader for a particular group. Name how the gifts will meet the needs of the class or group. If others have identified those gifts and recommended the teacher to you, share what you can of that information. Many of us seem to think that others don't see our gifts, and there is a certain power in having them named and called forth.

Give the prospective teachers time to think and pray. Encourage prospective teachers to pray for guidance as they consider your invitation and do not expect an answer on the spot. (In fact, do not accept an answer immediately.) Give the prospective teachers time to think and discuss the commitment with a spouse or other person who might be affected by the teacher's acceptance. If the answer is affirmative, thank them. If not, lovingly respect the decision. Make notes about ways to include them in leadership at a later date.

A COVENANT WITH EDUCATIONAL LEADERS
As a way to acknowledge formally the call of God in teachers' lives, work with your teachers to develop a covenant. Talk together about your vision for Christian education and formation as well as what is required of teachers and leaders in order for the vision to become reality. Ask teachers what they need from the congregation in order to be effective.

Then write down your agreement and have the teachers, pastor, and members of the ministry team sign the covenant. A sample agreement might include the following:
- Teachers and leaders will plan and prepare prayerfully.
- Teachers and leaders will participate in worship.
- Teachers and leaders will tend to their ongoing spiritual growth.
- The congregation will support teachers' and leaders' spiritual growth.
- The congregation will provide opportunities for teachers' and leaders' continued growth in knowledge and skills.
- The pastor and other congregational leaders will promote active participation in classes and other small groups and interpret the role of these classes and groups in developing Christian faith and discipleship.

Equipping and Supporting Teachers

Offer orientation-to-teaching sessions several times during the year. Invite potential teachers to explore whether teaching might be their gift.

Provide new teachers with information and assistance. Explain procedures for obtaining supplies, keeping attendance, collecting offerings, and other group needs. Furnish help with lesson planning and curriculum use. Remember Curric-U-Phone (1-800-251-8591), the toll-free help line for Cokesbury resources and Christian education planning.

Determine teachers' needs. Find out what knowledge and skills your teachers need to develop or strengthen and how to support their spiritual formation.

Provide ongoing opportunities for development. Plan to meet with your teachers once a quarter if possible. Schedule a presentation that addresses one of their expressed needs. Contact your conference or district office for names of people who can lead teacher development events. Also include a time for teachers to raise questions, identify concerns, and share advice and success stories.

TIP: In addition to teachers' meetings, plan for ways that teachers can increase their effectiveness individually. Provide articles, books, videos, and audiotapes related to teaching, the Bible, age-level development, and spiritual disciplines. Provide funds for online classes.

Express appreciation. There are many ways to say thank you. Consider which of these ideas might work for you:
- dedicating teachers and their work during a worship service
- holding a teachers' brunch, picnic, or covered-dish dinner
- sending thank-you notes
- writing newsletter articles that recognize the commitment of a teacher
- purchasing a book for the church library in honor of a teacher
- sponsoring a spiritual growth retreat
- establishing prayer partners for each group leader.

TIP: Provide childcare during teachers' meetings and other special events planned for teachers. You might also schedule times for leaders to come to the church for planning and preparing their rooms. Check to see if teachers need childcare during those planning times.

Find ways to give long-time teachers a Sabbath from teaching. Check with teachers each year to be sure they know they can take a break when they need to. Don't assume that all teachers will want or be able to return to a class year after year. Even Jesus needed a rest now and then. Arrange for an occasional substitute, an alternate teacher, or a team teacher to relieve teachers who need time off or help in order to continue.

Pray for your teachers. Above all, continue to pray for each teacher, for his or her students, and for your congregation.

BASIC RESOURCES FOR TEACHERS
Post a list of available resources for teachers in the church office, supply room, and church library. Distribute the resource list to teachers.

Basic resources include:
- Bible commentaries, such as the *New Interpreter's Bible*
- Bible dictionary, atlas, concordance
- children's illustrated Bible storybooks
- resources that describe age-level characteristics of children, youth, and adults
- books, videos, or DVDs that describe teaching methods
- devotional books and periodicals

Keeping Teachers Informed

Information and frequent communication build confidence and increase teachers' comfort levels. The following list of questions was created to help you anticipate the needs of the teachers and leaders in your church.

Meeting Space
- Where does the class or group meet?
- Are there restrictions on how the teachers may use or decorate the space?
- Do other groups use the same space at another time?

Time Schedules
- What time are group leaders expected to arrive?
- How long does each group meet?
- Will other groups be using the space immediately prior to or after this class?
- When can leaders prepare the space for their group?

Curriculum and Resources
- How do group leaders participate in selecting resources for their group?
- When and how do teachers receive their curriculum?
- Are extra materials available?
- What do teachers do with resources when finished with them?
- How do teachers provide input and evaluation of the resources?

Resources, Supplies, and Equipment
- What supplies are available?
- Does the church have media resources and audiovisual equipment? Where are they stored? How do teachers arrange to review media resources?
- Does the church have a library? Where is it?
- What is the procedure for checking out books, supplies, and equipment?
- When do teachers have access to resources and supplies?
- What if a teacher needs supplies the church doesn't have?
- Is there a budget to reimburse group leaders for out-of-pocket expenses?

Safety and Emergency Procedures

- Who is designated to pick up each member of a children's class or group?
- Have all teachers, helpers, and other volunteers who work with minors or other vulnerable participants had a background check?
- Do you have a "safe sanctuaries" policy in place and do all the teachers, leaders, and parents know about it? (See Resources.)
- Do you offer periodic "safe sanctuary" training? Do you have copies of *Safe Sanctuaries* for youth and children in your church library?
- What should a teacher do if he or she suspects that a group member is being abused? How do you help teachers to know this and other legal issues?
- How do teachers know if class members have any allergies or other medical conditions that might affect their participation in the group?
- Where is the first-aid kit?
- Where is the nearest available telephone?
- What is the telephone number for the nearest hospital?
- Where are the fire alarms and fire extinguishers located?
- What is the emergency evacuation plan?

Curriculum Resources

as well as planning the educational settings your congregation will provide, you have responsibility for identifying appropriate resources for each setting. The *Book of Discipline* requires the denomination to provide curriculum resources that conform to United Methodist theology, mission, and heritage that is described in the *Discipline*. That requirement implies that all United Methodist congregations will use these resources. The curriculum resources are expected to meet the criteria below.

With your ministry team, review the purpose of your educational ministries as you have come to understand it through study, conversation, and prayer. Identify the biblical and theological foundations that undergird your purpose. Restate what values, attitudes, behavior, knowledge, and skills you hope people will develop through participating in your congregation's ministry of Christian education.

AFFIRMING OUR MINISTRY

You may want to use the following quotation from *Foundations: Shaping the Ministry of Christian Education in Your Congregation* (pp. 6-7) when you identify criteria for choosing curriculum resources. Discuss how this quote identifies some of the results you hope will occur through your educational ministries. List any other results that are not evident in the quote.

"We believe in God, revealed through Jesus Christ, the Holy Spirit, and creation, as witnessed to through the scripture, the worship, and the traditions of the faith, and we affirm that all of us, through our participation in Christian education, will:
- Declare that God is present and active in the world;
- Know the content of the Bible and the Christian faith;
- Reflect on, discuss, witness to, and live our faith;
- Make decisions based on our Christian values;
- Discern and respond to the ministry to which God calls us;
- Grow in God's grace and in the gifts God has given us for ministry;
- Engage in a lifelong journey of learning and living the faith."

Selecting Resources

Forecast, an annual catalog describing all available United Methodist curriculum resources, is mailed every year to each local church. There are bi-monthly supplements for *Forecast* according to age level, and each catalog includes a curriculum order form. Free additional copies may be ordered from Cokesbury. Curriculum consultants are available through Curric-U-Phone: 800-251-8591.

With the conversation with your ministry team, these criteria may also assist you in identifying and selecting resources:
- The resource provides teachers with ideas to connect the Scripture with the daily lives of their group members.
- The resource supports teachers' spiritual formation.
- Instructions, when included, are clear and easy to follow.
- Group experiences include worship and other spiritual disciplines.
- Learning activities deepen knowledge of the Bible and of the Christian faith.
- Illustrations, when included, depict the diversity of all God's people.
- Group activities provide for a variety of learning styles.
- Group experiences create a loving, supportive group.
- Learning activities match the abilities of the age group for which they are planned.
- The resource fosters personal encounters with God's grace through Jesus Christ.
- Learning experiences develop attitudes of compassion, care, and hope.
- The resource provides opportunities to expand critical thinking skills.

- Group activities increase skills in living the faith and in serving others.
- Group activities inspire teachers and group members alike to commit their lives as disciples of Jesus Christ.

TIP: Before you purchase curriculum resources, preview samples at a Cokesbury bookstore or at Cokesbury.com. Your conference may have review copies in the media center. Check with other congregations in your area, particularly large churches, and ask if they have copies of any resources that you are considering.

Place orders for curriculum six to eight weeks prior to the date needed. You can order curriculum by mail, phone, or fax. Use the order form found in *Forecast* or order by phone Mondays-Fridays between 7:00 a.m. and 6:30 p.m., Saturdays 8 a.m. to 4 p.m. central time. Call toll-free 800-672-1789. Order by fax anytime: 800-445-8189. You can also order resources through Cokesbury online at http://www.cokesbury.com.

- *Forecast* (Cokesbury). An annual catalog of United Methodist curriculum resources and other helpful Christian education materials. Free from Cokesbury.
- Sunday School: It's for Life! Help for invigorating the Sunday school in all sized churches. http://www.sundayschool.cokesbury.com.
- Curriculum Finder is available at Sunday School: It's for Life!

Promoting Christian Education

everything teaches. The ministry of Christian education and formation enhances many, if not all, other ministry areas. How you promote and advocate for Christian education ministry is one indicator of the value placed upon it by the congregation. It is vitally important, therefore, to ask for, encourage, and enlist the support of the pastor and other professional staff of the church. When you plan for your communication about this ministry area, think about how the information will:

- build a shared vision for your teaching ministry
- build connections between Christian education and other areas of congregational life
- present information concisely and accurately
- encourage participation
- inspire appreciation for the significance of the teaching ministry.

TEN TIPS FOR PLANNING PUBLICITY

1. Use publicity to build a shared vision for Christian education.
2. Be as personal as possible; include how opportunities will benefit the intended audience.
3. Use at least two forms of publicity.
4. Repeat; be redundant!
5. Be uncomplicated in message and presentation.
6. Provide important details: what, when, where, for whom, cost.
7. Target your publicity for those who should participate.
8. Use the highest quality possible.
9. Include publicity in your budget.
10. Evaluate the publicity.

WORK THROUGH ESTABLISHED AVENUES

To begin, work through established avenues for publicity, such as:

Greeters. Using greeters or hosts and hostesses during times when you offer classes and small groups can create a direct and personal link to the congregation and is essential if you have guests visiting the church. These persons not only welcome those attending classes but they also act as a point of communication between the ministry team and individuals.

Reports. Make or send out a report, no matter how brief, at all church council meetings. The reports keep the church leaders informed of your plans and remind them of the importance of Christian education and formation.

Indoor and outdoor bulletin boards, signs, placards, banners, or posters. These easily-seen visual displays should be attractive, eye-catching, and people oriented. Change them at least once a month.

Opportunities at worship. Include some aspect of the church school in worship at least once a month. You might print a notice in the bulletin, provide a special insert, ask the pastor to include stories and songs currently being studied in classes in his or her sermon, ask a class to present a skit, or use a litany or prayer written by a church school class.

TIP: Plan to celebrate Christian Education Sunday sometime in September or on another Sunday of your choice. *Christian Education Week* is a free resource with ideas for theme, a teachers' workshop, worship suggestions, and reproducible clip art. It is available in English, Spanish, and Korean. Download from www.gbod.org/education or contact the General Board of Discipleship (877-899-2780, ext. 7053).

Church newsletters. In each issue write a column publicizing upcoming events or classes or recognizing a particular class or teacher. Since the pastor's column is frequently one of the most widely read pieces of direct mail, encourage him or her to refer to small groups and classes regularly.

Other print resources. In addition to the newsletter, make use of news stories, newspaper ads, and printed pamphlets that highlight different areas of your ministry.

Use of the membership rolls. When you are targeting a specific group for publicity, use your membership roll to identify all members of that specific group. Plan a direct mail publicity piece for those people or make personal telephone calls to them to discuss an opportunity designed for them.

Conference and congregational websites. Create links to information about your classes and small groups. Include specifics about location, time, and target audience. Provide the name of a contact person for each class and group in case interested persons want more information. Make use of both congregational and annual conference sites and links.

Electronic and media contacts. Use e-mail, telephone campaigns, direct mail, TV, or radio contacts.

Community outreach. Establish a presence at appropriate events and settings in the community, including having a booth or kiosk at public events (when permissible) and at church-wide events.

Regardless of the size of your congregation or the size of your budget, plan to publicize your educational ministries regularly. Even longtime members of the congregation need to be reminded of the opportunities available to them for learning and growing in faith.

Resources

** Denotes our top picks. (See also resources at www.gbod.org/education.)

LEADERSHIP

- **Christian Educators Fellowship (www.cefumc.org) is a professional national organization for leaders in Christian education and formation. Many annual conferences have a chapter.
- **Foundations: Shaping the Ministry of Christian Education in Your Congregation* (Nashville: Discipleship Resources, 1993. ISBN 978-0-88177-123-7). Provides guidelines for education in The United Methodist Church.
- *Guidelines for Leading Your Congregation:* Adult Ministries, Youth Ministries, Children's Ministries, Family Ministries (Nashville: Cokesbury, 2008.)
- *Keeping in Touch: Christian Formation and Teaching,* by Carol F. Krau (Nashville: Discipleship Resources, 1999. ISBN 978-0-88177-248-7). Suggests five critical processes for teachers and small group leaders.
- *Live, Learn, Pass It On!: The Practical Benefits of Generations Growing Together in Faith,* by Patty Meyers (Nashville: Discipleship Resources, 2006. ISBN 978-0-88177-469-6). An overview of intergenerational learning with models, practical helps, and biblical-theological foundations.
- ***Loving God With All Your Mind: Equipping the Community of Faith for Theological Thinking,* by Thomas R. Hawkins (Nashville: Discipleship Resources, 2004. ISBN 978-0-88177-398-9). Accessible resource on brain research, learning, and thinking.
- ***The Ministry of Christian Education and Formation: A Practical Guide for Your Congregation,* by the Christian education staff of the General Board of Discipleship (Nashville: Discipleship Resources, 2003. ISBN 978-0-88177-395-8).
- *The Nuts and Bolts of Christian Education,* by Delia Halverson (Nashville: Abingdon Press, 2000. ISBN 978-068707-116-6).
- *Sacred Challenge: Blazing a New Path for the Sunday School of the Future,* by Mike Ratliff (Nashville: Discipleship Resources, 2006. ISBN 978-0-88177-479-5). Uses Appreciative Inquiry to identify and to implement the core ministry of Christian education, especially through the church school.
- *Safe Sanctuaries for Youth: Reducing the Risk of Abuse in Youth Ministries,* by Joy Thornburg Melton (Nashville: Discipleship Resources, 2003. ISBN 978-0-88177-404-3). Helps churches assess risk and implement processes that reduce the likelihood of abuse in ministries with young people.

- *Safe Sanctuaries: Reducing the Risk of Child Abuse in the Church,* by Joy Thornburg Melton (Nashville: Discipleship Resources, 1998. ISBN 978-0-88177-220-3).
- *Santuarios seguros: Prevarición del abuso infantil y juvenil en la iglesia* by Joy Thornburg Melton; translated by Janette Marie Chevére (Nashville: Discipleshiup Resources, 2005. ISBN 978-0-88177-402-3)
- *Teaching Today's Teachers to Teach, Revised Edition,* by Donald L. Griggs (Nashville: Abingdon Press, 2003. ISBN 978-068704-954-7). This book is a basic, comprehensive manual offering practical guidance that helps teachers learn the art and practice of teaching.
- **Look for more teacher and teaching helps at www.gbod.org/education.

TEACHING AND LEARNING

- *Christian Education in the Small Membership Church,* by Karen Tye (Nashville: Abingdon Press, 2008. ISBN 978-068765-099-6). Invites pastors to lead their small membership churches to develop an imaginative and holistic vision of Christian Education.
- *The Church as Learning Community: A Comprehensive Guide to Christian Education,* by Norma Cook Everist (Nashville: Abingdon Press, 2002. ISBN 978-0-687-04500-6). Whenever and wherever Christians are being formed into the image of Jesus Christ through ministry, there Christian education is taking place.
- *Formation in Faith: The Congregational Ministry of Making Disciples,* by Sondra Mattaei (Nashville: Abingdon Press, 2008. ISBN 978-068764-973-0). While congregations know that disciple making is at the heart of their identity, they often have trouble understanding how to go about it.
- *I Knew Them All by Heart: The Legacy of a Sunday School Teacher,* by Myrtle Felkner (Nashville: Discipleship Resources, 2006. ISBN 0-88177-477-4. Inspirational and invigorating stories to refresh teachers.
- *iTeach*: monthly e-letter for teachers; www.gbod.org/education.
- *Our Spiritual Brain: Integrating Brain Research and Faith Development,* by Barbara Bruce (Nashville: Abingdon Press, 2002. ISBN 978-0-687-09266-6). How brain function affects teaching and learning.
- *Raising Children to Love Their Neighbors: Practical Resources for Congregations,* by Carolyn Brown (Nashville: Abingdon Press, 2008. ISBN 978-068765-142-9). For the congregation that wants to raise more mission-minded children.
- *Soul Stories: African American Christian Education, Revised Edition,* by Anne E. Streaty Wimberly (Nashville: Abingdon Press, 2005. ISBN 978-068749-432-3). Soul stories link persons' everyday life with the Christian Scriptures.
- *Triangular Teaching: A New Way of Teaching the Bible to Adults,* by Barbara Bruce (Nashville: Abingdon Press, 2007. ISBN 978-068764-352-3). Integrated, using multiple intelligence, brain research, and creativity.